Listen to the Sky

by Elaine Harris & Emily Veale

Are you ready to take a
JOURNEY together?

One that will leave you feeling
peaceful and RELAXED.

Are you lying nice and comfortable?

This would be a good time to make a WISH....
Maybe wish for something in your life that you would like to see happen!

If you like you could make the sound
"Ommmm."

Love

Can you think about your TUMMY?

Take a big BREATH into your tummy and fill it up like a balloon.

Suck a little more air in then BREATHE it out

"Ahhhhhh..."

Let your Tummy soften and RELAX.

Can you crunch your SHOULDERS
up to your ears?

Crunch, crunch, crunch……

Then RELAX your shoulders back down.

Now crunch your FACE up.
Close your EYES and squeeze your LIPS together.

Suck in your cheeks and SQUEEZE your whole
face together into the tip of your nose.
SQUEEZE more…….

Then RELAX your whole face.

Now lying really still without moving any part of your body, could you begin to RELAX your feet, all your toes, your whole legs, your hands, your fingers, your whole arms, your belly, your chest, your heart and your lungs.

The whole of your back is relaxed.

Could you relax your shoulders, neck, mouth, cheeks, ears, nose, eyes, forehead?

Your whole head is relaxed.

Can you notice the BREATH?
As you BREATHE IN and as you BREATHE OUT......

Maybe it is flowing like a gentle BREEZE....

Just listen to the sound of the BREATH.

Notice your mind.

Let the thoughts drift by like clouds in the sky.

If your mind WANDERS you can concentrate on the sound of your BREATH.

Can you notice how HEAVY
the whole body feels?

Maybe you can feel the EARTH underneath you
which is keeping you from falling.

Now feel the whole body getting
LIGHTER and LIGHTER......

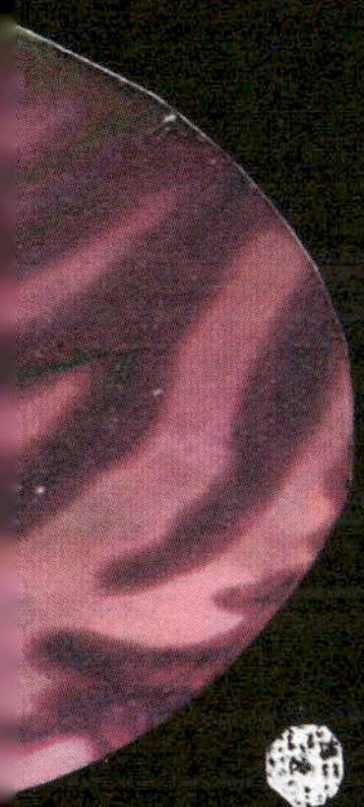

So light that you are
FLOATING into SPACE.

It is RAINING now and
big wet RAINDROPS
are making you feel COLD.

The rainshowers stop and a GOLDEN SUN is now coming through the clouds.

The GOLDEN SUNSHINE fills your whole body with warmth and you feel so HOT.

YOU notice a STORM out at SEA.

The WAVES are crashing and
the BOATS are bouncing up and down.

But you are SAFE and WARM indoors.

You can see a FIELD of GREEN GRASS
and a FARMYARD.

There is a FOREST of TALL TREES.

As you walk through the TREES you come to a magnificent **MOUNTAIN.**

From the top of the MOUNTAIN
you see a LIGHTHOUSE
sending a HUGE BEAM of YELLOW LIGHT
from the beacon.

This YELLOW LIGHT flows over
your whole body filling you with love.

The Light shines brightly over
all of your family and friends
filling them with love.

Everyone you know is covered
in the BEAUTIFUL BEAM of love.

The RAY of LIGHT stretches so long
that it shines on everyone in the WHOLE WORLD
filling everyone with love.

Can you listen to the SOUND of your HEART?

Hear the gentle RHYTHM of your HEARTBEAT.

FEEL the SPACE in your HEART
becoming bigger and bigger
as you are filled with LOVE and LIGHT.

Maybe you can notice how PEACEFUL you feel...

RELAX and ENJOY this PEACE.

Very slowly could you begin to notice any SOUNDS outside?

Listen to the NOISES that you hear.

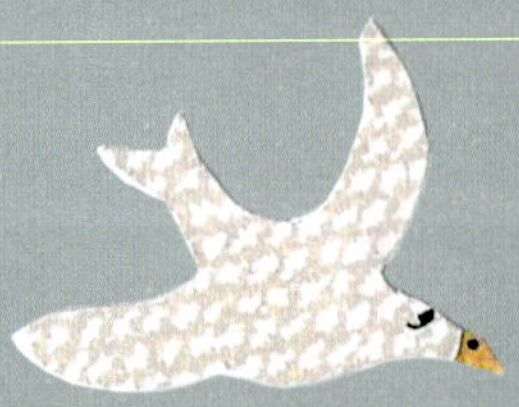

Listen to your BREATH once more.

Could you take a deep BREATH in?

And SIGH it out *Aaaaahhhhhhh*.

Think about your BODY again.

Gently **wiggle** your toes.
Gently **wiggle** your fingers.

Maybe you could STRETCH
your WHOLE BODY.

SLOWLY roll over onto your side and GIVE yourSELF a BIG HUG.

Notice how you FEEL now after being so relaxed.

Elaine Harris is a yoga teacher and writer. She has taught yoga to hundreds of children in Ireland, the UK and Australia.

She is the founder of The Yoga Shed which offers therapeutic yoga to children with special needs.

Elaine lives with her husband Damien and two children in Wicklow, Ireland.

For more information on Elaine's work see www.theyogashed.ie

Emily Veale is a collage artist and socially engaged practitioner living in Bray, Co. Wicklow.

She graduated from Fine Art Painting from NCAD in 2015 and is currently undergoing her MA in socially engaged art and further education in NCAD.

Her work consists of delicate hand collages created using found and recycled materials. Inspired by the everyday, the collages capture the vibrant and gentle atmosphere of her surroundings through a meditative approach.